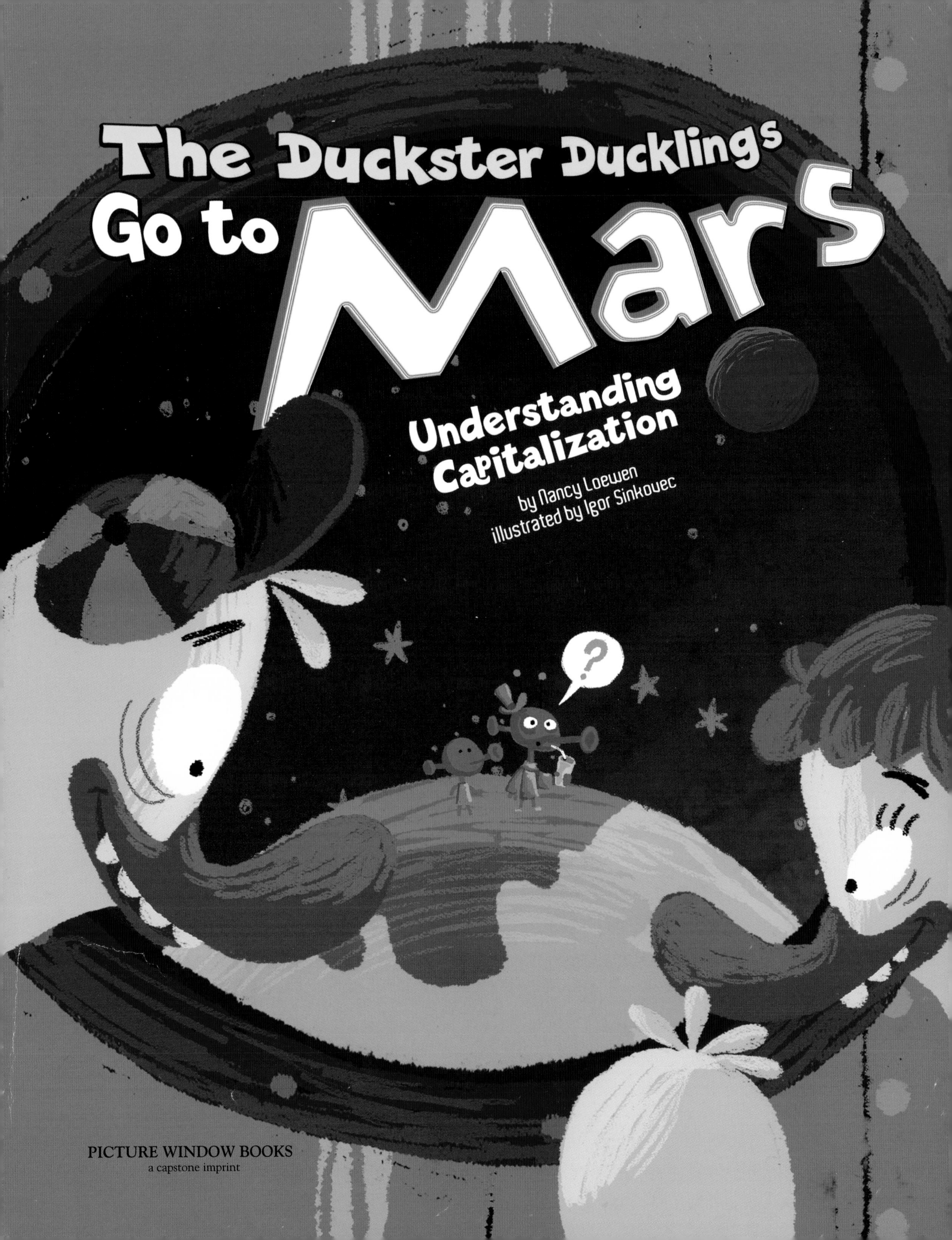

The Duckster Ducklings Go to Mars

Understanding Capitalization

by Nancy Loewen

illustrated by Igor Sinkovec

PICTURE WINDOW BOOKS
a capstone imprint

The Duckster family was special.
Boy, was that family going places.

On Fridays the Ducksters flew to
France to visit Grandpa Fred.

On Mondays in March,
they motored to Maine
to visit Aunt Mavis.

2

And on Saturdays in September, they swam to South America—just for something to do.

Normally the Duckster family was very well organized.

But one day—a Friday the 13th in June—things went haywire.

Mr. and Mrs. Duckster zigged while their ducklings zagged.

4

The ducklings kept on zagging until they reached the end of Cosmos Road. There they discovered something they'd never seen in all their travels.

A spaceship!

"Hello? Sir? Madam? Is anyone here?" asked Mae.

No one answered.

The ducklings tumbled inside.

"Cool!" said Buzz.

"Let us see," said John and Sally.

As the ducklings jostled, Christa fell beak-first onto the biggest button of all.

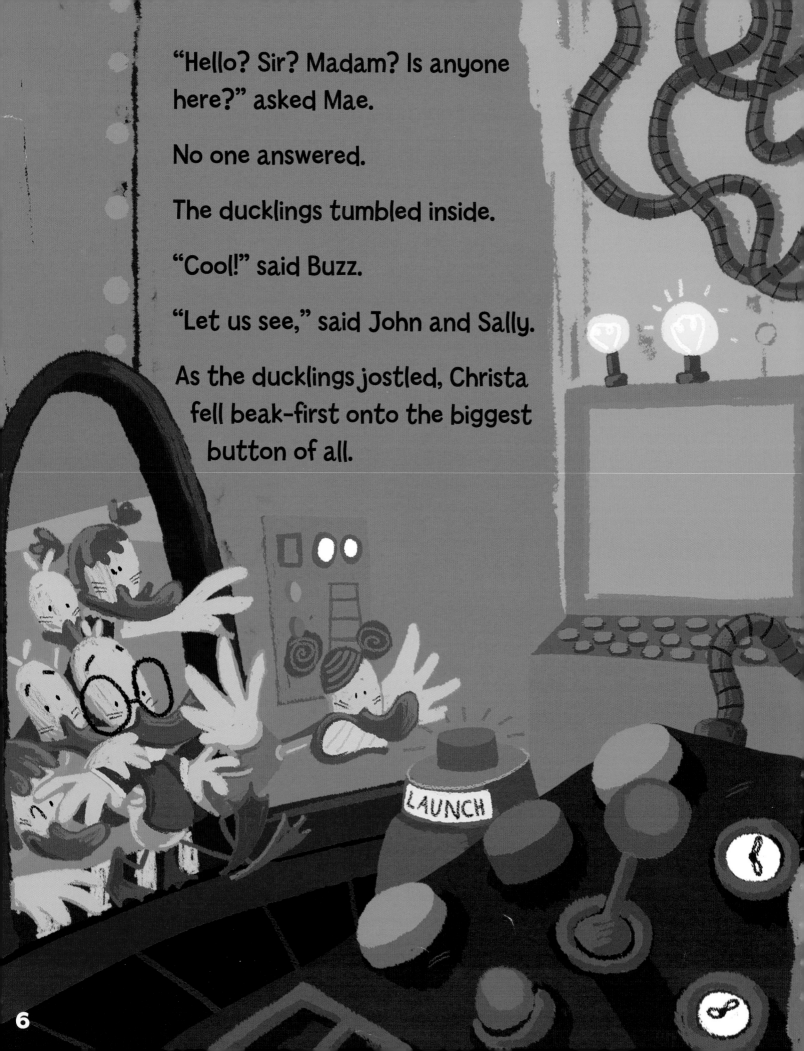

LAUNCH

The *Mars Express* began to rumble.
Then—WHOOSH!

The ducklings watched in amazement as Earth became a tiny blue speck beneath them.

Meanwhile Mr. and Mrs. Duckster searched high and low for their ducklings.

Days passed. The Duckster ducklings explored every inch of the *Mars Express*. They enjoyed the dazzling view.

But Mae was getting worried.

Going to Mars by ourselves is a big adventure and all, but how are we going to get back home?

Everyone stopped.

"Are we going to miss Groundhog Day?" whispered Buzz.

"And the Fourth of July?" asked Sally.

Neil teared up. "Will we ever see Mom and Dad again?"

Back on Earth Mr. and Mrs. Duckster received an urgent call. It was Director Smith, from the National Organization for Space Exploration and Yodeling (NOSEY).

Newspapers around the world carried the story.

Exclusive:
Are Ducklings
Spies?

Ducklings
Lost in
Space

News Report:
Ducks Out
of Luck?

KDUC'S
EYE to
the SKY

DUCKLINGS GO
TO MARS

TV reporters followed Mr. and Mrs.
Duckster wherever they went.

The Ducksters even met with President
Parker and Vice President Valdez.

But at night Mr. and Mrs. Duckster
looked into the sky ... and sighed.

Back on the *Mars Express*, the ducklings were starting to work together.

Christa and Neil studied a book called *The Art of Martian Flight*.

Mae and John watched a how-to DVD called *How to Train Your Spaceship*.

To keep the others in good spirits, Buzz and Sally sang songs such as "Six Little Ducks" and "When You Wish Upon a Star."

As the spaceship approached Mars, the ducklings allowed themselves one long look. Then they got busy—pressing buttons, turning knobs, and pushing levers.

The *Mars Express* stopped ...

spun around a few times ...

and—**WHOOSH!**—raced forward, toward Earth.

"Hooray! We did it!" the ducklings cheered.

Days passed. Mr. and Mrs. Duckster received another call from Director Smith.

"NOSEY radar shows that the spaceship has turned around," she said. "We will be watching the situation closely."

The Ducksters hugged each other and ordered another round of Boston cream pie.

The spaceship continued to race toward Earth.
The ducklings watched in amazement as the planet
became a huge, beautiful ball beneath them.

Then, with a whir and a clank, the spaceship landed.

"Now what?" asked John.

"Now we get LOUD!" said Christa. "C'mon! Crank out those quacks!"

QUACK QUACK

QUACK

QUACK

QUACK

The Ducksters' phone rang. It was Director Smith again. "The spaceship has landed safely on Prince Edward Island in Canada," she said. "We don't, however, know the exact location."

That's great news! Wait a minute—I think I hear something.

Me too! I'd know those quacks anywhere!

QU...
QUACK

So Mr. and Mrs. Duckster flew over the Atlantic Ocean and the Bay of Fundy.

They swam across the Northumberland Strait.

They followed the sound of the quacks until, just outside Charlottetown—

The Duckster family was reunited!

Grandpa Fred flew in from France.
Aunt Mavis motored over from Maine.
Even Vice President Valdez stopped
by for a bit.

Mae exclaimed ...

QUACK!

QUACK!

QUACK!

This is more
fun than
New Year's Eve!

QUACK!

QUACK!

QUACK!

... and the rest of the
Ducksters happily agreed.

About Capitalization

Capital letters are like signals. They get our attention, letting us know that certain words are important in some way. Here are the basic rules of capitalization:

Capitalize the first word in a sentence, no matter how small the word is. The capital letter is a sign that a new thought is being expressed. (See how the words "Capitalize," "The," and "See" start with a capital letter?)

Capitalize the personal pronoun "I." (See the speech bubble on page 9 for an example of Mrs. Duckster using "I.")

Capitalize proper names, which identify
a particular person ...
    John
    Buzz
    Duckster
place ...
    Cosmos Road
    Maine
    Mars
or business or organization.
    Patsy's Pie Shop

Capitalize titles of respect (Mrs., Mr., Ms., Miss) and family titles if they go before someone's name (Aunt Mavis, Grandpa Fred). Capitalize job titles as well (President Parker, Director Smith).

Capitalize days of the week, months, and holidays (Friday, June, Fourth of July).

Capitalize main words in the titles of books, movies, newspapers, and songs (*Understanding Your Rocket*, "When You Wish Upon a Star").

Capitalize the names of ships and spacecraft (*Mars Express*).

Capitalize acronyms. Acronyms are words formed from the first letters of the major words in a complex name. UFO, for example, is an acronym that stands for Unidentified Flying Object.

Capitalize words to show emphasis (I SEE THEM, QUACK).

Have YOU ever ridden in the Mars Express? Seen a UFO? Met Vice President Valdez on a sunny Sunday? I have!

Read More

Murray, Kara. *Capitalization and Punctuation.* Core Language Skills. New York: PowerKids Press, 2014.

Ruscoe, Michael. *Kick Ball Capitalization.* Grammar All-Stars. Writing Tools. Pleasantville, N.Y.: Gareth Stevens Pub., 2010.

Shaskan, Trisha Speed. *If You Were a Capital Letter.* Word Fun. Minneapolis: Picture Window Books, 2010.

Internet Sites

FactHound offers a safe, fun way to find Internet sites related to this book. All of the sites on FactHound have been researched by our staff.

Here's all you do:

Visit *www.facthound.com*

Type in this code: 9781479569663

Check out projects, games and lots more at
www.capstonekids.com

Special thanks to our adviser, Terry Flaherty, PhD, Professor of English, Minnesota State University, Mankato, for his expertise.

Editor: Jill Kalz
Designer: Ted Williams
Creative Director: Nathan Gassman
Production Specialist: Katy LaVigne
The illustrations in this book were created digitally.

Picture Window Books are published by Capstone,
1710 Roe Crest Drive, North Mankato, Minnesota 56003
www.capstonepub.com

Library of Congress Cataloging-in-Publication Data
Loewen, Nancy, 1964–
  The Duckster Ducklings go to Mars : understanding capitalization / by Nancy Loewen.
    pages cm.—(Picture window books. Language on the loose)
  Includes bibliographical references and index.
  Summary: "Introduces the concept of capitalization through the telling of an original story"—Provided by publisher.
  ISBN 978-1-4795-6966-3 (library binding)
  ISBN 978-1-4795-6970-0 (paperback)
  ISBN 978-1-4795-6974-8 (eBook PDF)
1. English language—Capitalization—Juvenile literature.
2. English language—Capitalization—Study and teaching (Elementary) I. Title. II. Title: Understanding capitalization.
PE1450.L63 2016
428.1'3—dc23   2014049207

Look for all the books in the series:

The BIG Problem (and the Squirrel Who Eventually Solved It)
Understanding Adjectives and Adverbs

The Duckster Ducklings Go to Mars
Understanding Capitalization

Frog. Frog? Frog!
Understanding Sentence Types

Monsters Can Mosey
Understanding Shades of Meaning

Sasha Sings
Understanding Parts of a Sentence

They're Up to Something in There
Understanding There, Their, and They're

whatever says mark
Knowing and Using Punctuation

When and Why Did the Horse Fly?
Knowing and Using Question Words

Printed in the United States of America in North Mankato, Minnesota.   052015   008823CGF15